THE WORLD'S LAST STEAM LOCOMOTIVES IN INDUSTRY

THE 21ST CENTURY

GORDON EDGAR

AMBERLEY

Right: At dawn on 30 December 2002, Pingdingshan Coal Railway QJ 2-10-2 7186 blows down before moving onto the depot for servicing, as JS 2-8-2 5644 waits to leave Tianzhuang yard with empty coal wagons.

Front cover: In the vast opencast mine at Sandaoling on 16 January 2016, JS Datong works 1987-built Class 2-8-2s No.8167 waits to set back to the 'blue loader' at Xikeng, as No.8225 slowly but surely gets to grips with its 13-wagon loaded train at the start of the steep ascent out of the pit to one of two discharge points.

Back cover: Following water replenishment, Yugoslav 'USA' 0-6-0 tank 62-111 heads back to its task of positioning wagons alongside a shovel loader at Durdevik mine in Bosnia-Herzegovina on 26 February 2015.

First published 2023

Amberley Publishing
The Hill, Stroud
Gloucestershire, GL5 4EP

www.amberley-books.com

ISBN 978 1 3981 0810 3 (paperback)
ISBN 978 1 3981 0811 0 (ebook)

British Library Cataloguing in Publication Data.
A catalogue record for this book is available from the British Library.

Typeset in 10pt on 12pt Sabon LT Std.
by SJmagic DESIGN SERVICES, India.
Printed in Great Britain.

CONTENTS

INTRODUCTION AND ACKNOWLEDGEMENTS

This title concludes my series of photographic books featuring industrial railways, and what an enjoyable 'journey' it has been in creating them, one that initially started out with a photographic study of Hunslet 'Austerity' locomotives, followed by a series of regional books looking back at the British industrial railway scene, primarily over the last half-century, with its rich variety of locomotives, track gauges, and industrial environments. Finally, 'travelling' overseas to review the last vestiges of working industrial steam in the last four decades or so. It has been an immensely pleasurable task compiling these books, and no less so with this edition, but I must admit to having suffered from some mixed emotions whilst working on this latest title, the final one in a series of thirteen books covering an industrial railway theme. I have been extremely fortunate to have visited some far flung and obscure places in the world in search of steam over the last two decades or more, especially to some provinces of China where the usual globetrotting tourist would never have contemplated setting foot. There have been many rewarding and thought-provoking experiences along the way, making many good friends and acquaintances. Choosing suitable photos for inclusion here has been an absorbing experience and has certainly rekindled many happy memories. Conversely, the associated research undertaken to accompany the captions has astonished me, more so than at the time of the actual events unfolding, just how quickly the momentum gathered during steam's demise. This was no more evident than in China, where the standard industrial SY Class 'Mikado' was still being constructed right up until 1999, perhaps creating a false conception that they would be 'clanking around' mines and steelworks systems for many years hence.

As the new millennium unfolded, the scope for world industrial steam photography was still relatively broad, and the range of places to choose from for potential visits, to which only a limited amount of free time could be devoted, posed something of a dilemma. It soon became clear that the writing was truly on the wall for steam, even in China, so it was inevitable that the few surviving steam-worked systems in other parts of the world could end up being by-passed, or perhaps only visited during their eleventh hour. The sheer number of noteworthy industrial systems in China still retaining steam around the new millennium was phenomenal, hence its domination in this book, and arguably quite rightly so.

I should emphasise that I am merely a photographer, and not a technical expert on the subject, so this is unashamedly a photographic book, with as much accompanying caption detail as space permits. The decision over which subjects to cover, whilst striking an acceptable balance between book size, image format, and caption detail has proved to be a challenging prospect. Unless otherwise stated, locomotives and their systems featured are of standard gauge, or 'Cape Gauge' in the case of Southern Africa. Some systems and their locomotives appeared to be 'main line' in nature, and in some cases the railway administrations acquired surplus main line steam locomotives, and this was most evident in China and Southern Africa. Most photos are of 'real steam', and not chartered workings endeavouring to recreate authentic workings; however there are a small number of exceptions included for completeness, namely those taken in Myanmar and Romania, plus a small number in Java, which I have annotated as such in the respective captions.

Conventional industrial steam has quite recently come to an end in Zimbabwe and Java, and China is more than likely to end the same way during 2022, leaving Bosnia-Herzegovina and possibly a steelworks in North Korea standing alone in the world where industry regularly relies on conventional (non-fireless) steam traction. The release of this book at such a watershed moment is a tribute to its final years in history, including wherever possible as much historical detail of their final workings or system closures as can be established. To that end, I am indebted to the excellent websites of Rob Dickinson's *International Steam*, Duncan Cotterill's *Railography*, Dave Fielding's *SY Country*, and Bernd Seiler's *FarRail Tours*. Without these extremely informative websites, supported by the detailed information submitted by many contributors over the decades and my own notes, the working status and consequent fate of the locos and their railway systems featured would have been inconclusive.

I am especially indebted to Darryl Bond, Warwick Falconer, Nick Pigott, John Sloane, Richard Stevens, and Don White for contributing photos to this book, without which certain railways, or indeed countries, could not have been featured, and I have credited accordingly those contributors in the captions. All other photos without any credit in the caption are of my own taking. It will be noted that some photographs taken are of workings before the new millennium, particularly in the cases of Cuba and India, however the locomotives and specific railways featured were still very much active into the 21st century.

At sunset on 12 January 2002, SY1255 storms away from Da Long colliery with a loaded coal train on the Tiefa system.

I would like to thank Richard Stevens for reviewing the draft copy of this book, although I accept full responsibility for any errors that may have crept in. Finally, and by no means least, I would like to thank my wife Valerie for her support and patience over the eight year period when I have been engaged in producing this industrial series, and for her kind understanding whenever I have chosen to disappear for lengthy periods of time to fulfil my passion for photographing everyday working industrial steam, which is not only out of reach as I write this, but sadly facing total extinction.

Gordon Edgar
Ripon, North Yorkshire

1
GERMANY

Representative of over 200 GDR Meiningen 0-6-0 fireless locos built, *F67* (W/No.03067 of 1985), owned by Romonta GmbH, heads from the Amsdorf factory, alongside the DB Halle– Nordhausen main line, with empty coal wagons for the DB exchange sidings at Röblingen am See, in the coal mining district of Mansfeld-Südharz on a wet and heavily overcast 27 October 2008. Established in 1922, Romonta operates its own opencast coal mine to extract lignite to produce Montan wax. Until 1995, when the company installed conveyor belts, it operated an extensive works and mines railway system and owned other wax production facilities and briquette factories in the area.

It is quite probable that the last steam locos to work in industrial service in the world will be of the fireless variety, and no country has more active examples than those remaining in Germany. Unconventional, and universally disliked by railway followers, they have been included for the sake of completeness. For decades, fireless locos have provided a versatile and cost-effective solution for companies producing a generous excess steam supply and requiring their own shunting loco. Germany has a long history of fireless loco construction, going as far back as 1882, when the Hohenzollern locomotive works supplied their first examples to a tramway in Java. One century later, locos of a similar but contemporary design were still under construction in Germany at Meiningen works. In the 1980s, this works manufactured 202 examples of a standard East German six-coupled type. Following reunification of Germany, some found use in the wider Federal Republic and Austria, replacing many of the older surviving locos still working. At the time of writing, five German companies were using fireless locos: at the Felix Schoeller paper factory in Osnabrück-Lüstringen, with Ineos Solvents at Herne in the Ruhr, at Mannheim power station alongside the Rhine in Baden-Württemberg, in Saxony-Anhalt at the Stassfurt soda factory, and at the Romonta wax factory at Amsdorf. Remarkably, Mannheim's coal-fired power station uses an eight-coupled 1955 Henschel-built example, brought out of 'retirement' from Gelsenkirchen-Bismarck railway museum and overhauled at Meiningen works in 2015. Elsewhere in Europe and for the record, fireless locos are still employed at Mondi paper factory in Ulmerfeld-Hausmening, near Linz in Austria, and at Ljubljana power station in Slovenia.

On 27 October 2008, the crew connect Meiningen works-built 0-6-0 fireless *F67* (W/No.03067 of 1985) to the steam charger at the Romonta wax factory following a trip to the DB exchange sidings.

Hoechst A. G. at Gendorf-Kastl in Upper Bavaria, was founded in 1939, for the manufacture of military-grade chemical products and was known to have used forced labour during the war period, including prisoners from the nearby Dachau concentration camp. The factory was dismantled after the war, and from 1955 the site was developed as a chemicals industrial park by Hoechst. Three fireless locos were used until March 2005, when regular shunting was taken over by diesels. During a visit on 17 May 1983, wartime-built Esslingen 0-6-0 fireless *Resi 2* (W/No.4691 of 1944) was positioning a loaded chemical tanker wagon on the plant's weighbridge. *Resi 2* was the oldest loco in the Hoechst fleet, later joined in 1951 by two new Krauss-Maffei fireless locos. The venerable 'Kriegslok' fireless *Resi 2* was subsequently held in reserve to diesel traction, and its last confirmed use was in March 2013.

2
ROMANIA

At dawn on a misty Saturday 8 October 2016, Reșița 1954-built 0-8-0 tank 764-421 makes up a morning train in the yard at Viseu de Sus, passing an arc welder going about his routine work outside the railway's workshop.

In the 1970s, Romania was one of the last countries in Europe where 760mm gauge forestry railways were still operating on a significant scale. Even in the late 1980s, fifteen such systems totalling around 1,000kms of route miles were remaining. However, this situation was to change rapidly, and by the new millennium there was just one operational system which still used steam traction. The country's poor economy post-1990 had a devastating impact on the state-run forestry railways, resulting in decommissioning and closure of most.

One of the last survivors was the run-down operation based at Viseu de Sus, located close to the border with Ukraine. Privatised in 1999, the first operating company went bankrupt in 2003, but its successor company, R. G. Holz Company, has since turned the operation around, transforming it into a thriving concern by introducing regular tourist trains to supplement the income from its ever-dwindling logging operation. This was a logical step to take in this increasingly popular tourist region of the Carpathians, particularly in the light of the ever-stricter regulations limiting deforestation. In doing so, the railway has taken on the unique dual status as both that of a tourist attraction and a traditional Romanian logging business. Its 760mm gauge main running line climbs for around 40km from Viseu, through the often narrow Vaser valley, deep into the forests of the Maramures Mountains, and on to the isolated logging community at Coman. The railway operation today relies on 1970s-built diesel-hydraulic locos, but most tourist trains are hauled by steam, and the photos of steam-hauled freight workings in this chapter were all chartered. There are still traditional logging methods used in some inaccessible forestry locations, where working horses haul logs to the railway loading points. Until as recently as 2004, the wood-burning 0-8-0 tanks saw daily use for shunting the Viseu sawmill yard, and they can still be called upon to move empty timber bogies up the line to loading points, for shunting around the Viseu woodyard whenever required, or even taking charge of a loaded train if necessary. Steam can also replace diesel traction if the fuel is temporarily unavailable, or is too expensive to procure. The timber fuel for the steam locos is freely available from the woodyard of course! Based on a 1900s Austro-Hungarian design, 120 of the '764' Class 0-8-0 tanks were built between 1951 and 1984 at Reșița Steelworks, and twelve were subsequently built at the Reghin tractor factory between 1984 and 1988. Perfectly at home working on steep gradients, sharp curves, and poor trackwork through the forests, they are fitted with spark arresting balloon stacks to mitigate the extreme fire hazard that they would otherwise pose.

In the depths of an intensely harsh winter in the Carpathian Mountains on 27 February 2018, a permanent way ganger steps aside as 764-421 passes, heading an empty logging train for loading at Suligu. This section is between Bardau and Botizu, 26km from Viseu, and is where the railway twists and turns through a deep, rocky valley.

Left: On 16 March 2015, the sun had dipped behind the hills and the light had begun to fade in the Vaser Valley near Valea Scradei, as Reşiţa 1954-built 0-8-0 tank 764-408R made cautious progress down the valley with the day's 'production train' for the Viseu sawmill, comprising fifteen loaded timber bogies and other assorted vehicles from the Bardau loading point.

Opposite page: On 15 March 2015, Reşiţa 1954-built 0-8-0 tank 764-435 shunts loaded timber bogies at Suligu yard, 30km from Viseu. This load would form part of the train for the Viseu railhead and sawmill during the following day, hauled by sister loco 764-408R.

Right: Complete with its animal passengers comprising two dogs and a working horse, a 'support train' heading for Coman on 16 March 2015 waits for a clear section, as Reşiţa 0-8-0 tank 764-408R *Cozia 1* drifts into Bardau in charge of a loaded log train from Suligu. Forestry workers are waiting to board their mixed 'support train' headed up front and out of view by a small 0-6-0 diesel-hydraulic loco.

On 26 February 2015, by then a rare occurrence, Class 62 0-6-0 tank 62-111 blackens the sky as it positions wagons for loading at RMU Durdevik colliery, near Zivinice. The colliery temporarily reinstated rail traffic when nearby Dubrave was out of commission, but subsequently the 4km branch linking Durdevik colliery with the main line at Zivinice fell into disuse.

3

BOSNIA-HERZEGOVINA

Bosnia-Herzegovina could quite possibly be the last country in the world to use conventional steam in a commercial industrial setting daily, until such time as Tuzla's power plant ceases to burn coal, or if sufficient funds are forthcoming for replacement diesel traction with a cost-effective fuel supply. Regular steam usage in this country is now restricted to shunting the two opencast mine loading points (LPs) on the fringes of Tuzla, to the north at Sikulje, and to the south at Dubrave, with one loco in use at each opencast LP's sidings. The Kreka Coal Mining Administration has a ready supply of 'free' fuel for its 1940s veteran 'Kriegslok' 2-10-0s, and the three-yearly heavy overhaul programme of each loco was still being carried out during 2022. Tuzla power station is also supplied with coal from the RMU Banovici mines, but use of steam is now irregular at the Oskova washery, which has both standard and 760mm gauges. Two 0-6-0 tanks, a Skoda Class 19 and a Class 62, are held in reserve, and at least until 2018, one of these would be used for shunting the brown coal processing plant and washery sidings whenever the diesel loco was under repair, or during the diesel loco's periodical eleven-day inspection. On the 760mm gauge line from the mines at Grivice, regular steam activity using either a Českomoravská Kolben-Daněk (ČKD) 1947-built 0-6-0 tank, or one of two Class 83 0-8-2 tender locos, had possibly ceased by 2018. In latter years, these locos had been restricted to around the clock working of rakes of side-discharge hopper wagons over the coal discharge bunker at Oskova, loaded trains being brought in over the 5km double track 'main line' by 1970-built Bo-Bo diesel-hydraulics. In recent summer months, these diesels have been prone to overheat on the stop-start duties at the tippler, and steam has consequently been reinstated on these occasions.

On 26 February 2013, during one of the rare movements that week when production at the Dubrave LP had ceased in the aftermath of an earthquake, which resulted in the death of coal thieves illegally operating overnight in the opencast pit, 33-064 was captured hauling loaded wagons out of the loader, subsequently placing them on one of the despatch sidings. No further movements were seen during the rest of the week, despite much time and effort being devoted to observation. Such was the challenge of photographing industrial steam well into the 21st century.

Above: On 9 November 2014, 33-064 storms away from Lukavac yard towards Sikulje LP with empties originating from the Tuzla power plant, and deposited earlier by a main line (ZFBH) diesel. The traditional Yugoslavian Railways semaphore signals protect access to Lukavac yard from the west.

Opposite page: Against the heavily polluted sky at Lukavac on 11 November 2014, 33-064 heads its rake of loaded four-wheel wagons past the by-products and coking plant. A local resident, her home adjoining the noxious industrial complex, returns to her residence from the corner shop with a daily newspaper, and waits for the train to pass, sensibly keeping her distance as scavengers on the wagons drop full sacks along the lineside, for gathering up later. They would then distribute them via the lucrative local 'black market' network.

Above: On 13 November 2014, 33-064 leaks steam and slips violently on the climb into Lukavac ZFBH exchange yard with its heavy load from Sikulje LP. The signalman displays his lamp from the cabin and the by-products plant illuminates the sky on this damp and slightly misty evening. The coal thieves riding on the loaded wagons go about their blatant but risky routine of filling their bags on the short journey, diligently observed but conveniently ignored by the railway authorities and police alike.

Opposite page: During the evening of 9 November 2014, the signalman stands at his post with an illuminated lamp, confirming a clear road ahead to the crew of 33-064 for its departure for the Sikulje LP sidings. With cylinder drain valves open, the eighty-year-old 'Kriegslok' confidently shifts its rake of empties away from Lukavac yard.

Left: Leaking steam profusely, ex-works 33-504 lifts a load away from Sikulje LP, eagerly paced by a feral dog, on 24 February 2015. The coal scavengers of the Roma community, who live in an adjacent rudimentary encampment, have already launched themselves into action precariously riding on the wagons, hastily filling as many bags as possible, despite the overt police observation. This entire area, including the opencast workings, became flooded in 2014 and the banking to the left was subsequently built to reduce similar future events.

Right: On 8 November 2014, 33-248 moves a rake of loaded wagons away from the loader at Dubrave. Such modest shunting movements are now the sole remaining regular conventional steam duties in this country, if not very soon in the entire world.

The 5km branch from the Dubrave LP to the main line at Ljubace crosses two automated level crossings. During the late afternoon of 8 November 2014, a dishevelled 33-248 crosses the first, intersecting with the Zivinice–Loznice–airport road. The 'dustbin lid' baffle on the loco's chimney frustratingly prevented a vertical exhaust, but the unseasonably warm conditions and the level branch line would not have resulted in any appreciable exhaust anyway. This coal was destined for Ljubace exchange sidings, for onward transit by a main line diesel to Tuzla power plant, but since 2016 the diesels have worked these trains along the branches to both the Dubrave and Sikulje LPs.

Above: All replacement parts for the ageing 'Kriegslok' fleet are machined at Bukinje. On 25 February 2015, redundant Class 62 0-6-0 tanks 62-376 and 62-368 dumped at the adjacent closed mine are visible through the machine shop window, as a machinist goes about his precision work of manufacturing parts for 33-248, then visiting the works for its three-yearly heavy overhaul.

Left: On 7 November 2014, two not very well-protected fitters cut new boiler tubes to size inside Bukinje workshops for 33-504 standing behind, with its boiler raised and wheels removed.

Opposite page: On 25 February 2015, the two spare 2-10-0s, 33-064 and 33-503, stand in the rain in the Bukinje works yard. 33-503 was receiving running repairs to pipework, before its rotation at either Dubrave or Sikulje with a sister loco requiring a washout and routine maintenance.

On the wet morning of 26 February 2015, Đuro Đakovic works 1956-built Class 62 0-6-0 tank 62-111 struggles to make progress along the steeply graded branch line with empties for Durdevik deep mine. This was a temporary period of demand by Tuzla power plant, due to the interruption of supplies from the nearby Dubrave opencast, which had suffered from earthquake damage during the previous week.

In between working the branch line, and positioning wagons beneath the loading screens on 26 February 2015, 'USA' 0-6-0 tank 62-111 takes on water alongside the Durdevik colliery buildings. The ground had become saturated with the thaw of a heavy snowfall from two weeks previously, which was immediately followed by a prolonged period of heavy rainfall.

During the evening of 23 February 2015, RMU Banovici's 760mm gauge 0-6-0 tank 25-30 gives a final push to a hopper wagon rake, following its discharge at the Oskova washery tipping dock. With the wagon brakes pinned down by the ground shunter, the 1947-built standard Yugoslavian industrial tank, built by ČKD in Prague, would then uncouple and set back light, before heading on the adjoining line to the reception sidings to collect the next load awaiting tipping. Meanwhile, the tipping dock labourers would be taking a well-earned break in their bothy before the next load required their attention. The entire external tipping area, with thick slurry underfoot, demanded stout waterproof footwear, and extreme vigilance amidst the bustling operations on this cold and wet night.

On 4 November 2014, with the daytime temperature rapidly rising to 23C, exhaust from the Class 83 loco proved to be minimal unless it was being fired. Former Yugoslavian Railways Đuro Đakovic 1948-built 0-8-2 83-158, fresh out of a full overhaul, moves freshly discharged hopper wagons away from the tipping dock at Oskova washery.

Left: During this visit, three different 760mm gauge steam locos were working Oskova washery over two consecutive days, with two required in traffic on both of those days, such was the winter demand for coal. On 23 February 2015, ČKD 1947-built 0-6-0 tank 25-30 had just replaced 0-8-2 83-158 on tipping dock duties. The tank loco gradually edged down the grade as each of the operators manually released the wagons' side doors to effect coal discharge.

Opposite page: On 14 March 2014, Class 62 0-6-0 tank 62-633 was attempting to get its train on the move at the start of the day, to access the decrepit colliery loading bay at Rudnik Zenica. Following the recent flooding, steam activity at the colliery was an irregular occurrence, and on borrowed time, this being the sole surviving active steam loco in the once heavily industrialised steel and coal mining town of Zenica, 75km north of Sarajevo. (Warwick Falconer)

Right: Climbing the steep grade on 27 February 2015, 25-30 undertakes a wagon positioning move between Oskova washery and the company's running shed and workshops at Banovici, passing the modest LP serving Banovici deep mine.

4

SERBIA

The state-owned Kolubara Group mine, near Vreoci, established in the 1950s, was Serbia's largest. On 28 May 2007, 62-643, one of two Class 62s usually in daily use, was busy at the washery loading point. New diesel locos arrived during 2008, putting an end to the last active industrial Class 62s in Serbia. (John Sloane)

A visit to Serbia, in the former Yugoslavia, in 2000 would have found seventeen steam locos seeing frequent work in a variety of traditional industrial settings. However, soon into the early 21st century, a more depressing scene was to unfold, with the remaining serviceable steam locos either being set aside in favour of diesel traction, or simply made redundant due to companies ceasing production following the general business downturn in the country after the Yugoslav Wars. Up until 2002–2003, a small handful of the once ubiquitous Yugoslav 'USA' Class 62 0-6-0 tank locos continued to see work, one woebegone example shunting the Smederovo Carriage and Wagon Workshops until May 2002, but an arguably more interesting operation was one

to be found at the 'Mose Pijada' cable factory in Jagodina, where one of three 'USA' tanks there was retained to work alongside a diesel on the workers' passenger trains, which were provided free of charge before and after each of the three shift changes. A short branch line linked Jagodina bus and railway station with the factory, and passenger accommodation was provided in vintage four-wheel balcony coaches, which the 62 usually hauled bunker-first away from the factory, and returned by propelling the coaches along the entire branch from Jagodina to the factory. Following the termination of night-shift work in 2002, one serviceable 62 was held in reserve to the diesel, until its boiler certificate expired. Even fireless locos in the country did not fare any better; a Class 62 tank, rebuilt for fireless operation at Lucani explosives factory, near Čačak, and the two Belgian 1956-built LaMeuse six-coupled locos used at the Loznica 'Viskoza' man-made fibres factory, were all out of use by 2003.

The 9km long 900mm gauge electrified line, serving a complex of four opencast mines at Vreoci, was worked by a fleet of twenty 1940s-design East German EL3 Class locos, but a fleet of four Class 53 Decauville 0-6-0 tank locos of that gauge had been used for shunting at the washery. On this 28 May 2007 visit, 53-017 was the last serviceable member of the class, but only retained in a reserve capacity. (John Sloane)

Former Hungarian Railways (MAV) 1893-design mixed traffic Class 325 0-6-0 126-014 was one of two of this veteran class held in reserve at Resavica mine, but neither had seen regular use for several years by the time of this visit in May 2007. (John Sloane)

Left: The Kostolac opencast mine at Drmno holds one of the largest reserves of lignite in Europe. The Klenovik opencast mine, part of the large complex, used a 900mm gauge steam-worked system, with an impressive semi-roundhouse for its fleet of five Davenport 1946-built post-WWII United Nations Relief & Rehabilitation Administration (UNRRA) 0-8-0s. Only two were latterly in regular use, chiefly during the winter months of increased coal demand at the Kostolac 'A' power station, connected to the narrow-gauge system. The railway was closed and lifted in April 2009, but two years previously one of its two serviceable 0-8-0s, No.13, was active, and is seen at the power station tipping dock with a rake of side-tipping wagons. (John Sloane)

Right: At the Resavica mine in May 2007, and held in reserve along with 126-014 was this former MAV Class 370 0-6-0, 120-019. The late 19th century veteran could only be used with a limited boiler pressure by this time. (John Sloane)

Cuba's chief trading partner, the Soviet Union, had propped up its sugar industry for over three decades, but the fall of the Union in 1991 caused a severe crisis in the Cuban economy. Consequently, from the mid-1990s the Cuban state invested heavily in promoting tourism, whilst reducing its reliance on the sugar industry. From around the 1980s, news was getting around in steam enthusiast circles about the remarkable fleet of veteran American steam locos on four gauges used by the Cuban sugar industry, administered by the state's Sugar Ministry (MINAZ). Operations on these railways supported the cane harvesting season (*zafra*), taking place during the first three to four months of every year, but activity on them could be unpredictable, influenced by the demands of the industry, some mills even closing for a complete season, only to reopen during the following year. The cheap low quality home-produced oil burned by most of the steam fleet ensured their longevity, with many eighty years old or more towards the end of the 20th century. By the new millennium, the writing was clearly on the wall for the Cuban sugar industry and, following the completion of the 2003 *zafra*, many mills experienced sudden closure, leaving only a handful still relying on an increasingly unreliable and dwindling steam fleet, and some mills had already been dieselised by that time. Some of the redundant and more dependable 2-8-0s were transferred to mills using the less powerful 2-6-0s, taking over the heavier cane trains between the loading point (*acopio*) and mill (*central*), as well as covering some 'inter-mill' duties over the national railway's metals (Ferrocarriles de Cuba – F.C.C.), leaving the surviving 'Moguls' to undertake less arduous tasks at the mill reception sidings (*patio*). Despite an ever dwindling number of working steam locos as each season passed, a handful of mills continued to rely on steam, but they were diminishing in number every year until, by the 2007 *zafra*, just one solitary standard-gauge steam loco was to see daily use in the island's sugar industry. Although the author took these photos during the 1998 *zafra*, all the mills featured experienced industrial steam activity in the early part of the 21st century.

Right: Baldwin 2-6-2 saddle tank 1343 (W/No.24614 of 1904) resting between duties at the servicing point of Marcelo Salado mill, Villa Clara Province. It was a remarkable survivor even by this visit on 8 April 1998, but it continued its mill 'switching' work until 2001. Located close to the historic town of Remedios, Marcelo Salado had a reputation for turning out smartly presented locos, and was one of the few mills still using tank locos during the final years of steam in Cuba.

5

CUBA

Left: At midday on 5 April 1998, Baldwin 2-8-0 1804 (W/No.52245 of 1919) was simmering between work in the oil-caked depot at Amistad con los Pueblos mill (literally 'Friendship with the Peoples'), in La Habana Province. This mill rarely opened, but until 2002 its locos continued to find 'inter-mill' work taking cane grown locally over the F.C.C. for processing at other mills.

Right: Gregorio Arlee Manalich mill had a reputation for periodically turning out its locos in a smart new livery. On 5 April 1998, 2ft 6in gauge Baldwin 2-8-0 1307 (W/No.53685 of 1920) rests between duties wearing an appropriate rich chocolate livery for this La Habana Province mill. Use of steam on the narrow gauge ceased after the 2004 season at this, the last Cuban mill to use steam traction on two gauges. Steam traction found work on the standard gauge until 2007.

On 17 April 1998, Vulcan Ironworks 2-8-0 1806 (W/No.2898 of 1918) blackens the surrounding countryside as it tackles the sharp grade from the south line to Boris Santa Coloma mill, in La Habana Province. Nicknamed 'the mill on the hill' and originally part of the Hershey chocolate empire, field lines connected the mill from the north and south, both with tortuous ascents for loaded trains. The mill also enjoyed a connection with the Ruben Martinez Villena system, but sadly regular steam activity ceased after the 2001 *zafra*.

On 6 April 1998, Baldwin 2-8-0 1605 (W/No.54051 of 1920) raises the echoes and disturbs the dust as it passes the magnificent building in the *patio* area at Ruben Martinez Villena mill, La Habana Province, with a loaded train on the truncated running line from the *acopio*, by this time supplied from the fields by road vehicles. This mill was renowned for having a remarkable and varied fleet, including the only two surviving coal-fired tank 'switcher' locos in the country. Steam was employed on 'inter-mill' working upon the mill's closure, but this ceased after the 2001 *zafra*.

Baldwin 2-6-0 1610 (W/No.58800 of 1925) was one of a trio of consecutively built locos supplied to Cuba Libre mill, in Matanzas Province, remaining there until the end of its limited steam operations by the end of the 2002 *zafra*. It is seen in charge of a heavy load from the Pedrosa *acopio*, approaching the reversal station at the F.C.C. station at Navajas on 6 April 1998.

Left: Baldwin 2ft 6in gauge 2-8-0 1355 (W/No.53864 of 1920) preparing to move off shed after the crew's lunch break at Mal Tiempo mill, Cienfuegos Province, on 7 April 1998. The final season of conventional steam activity here proved to be 2002, but by then the railway was rapidly experiencing a transformation into a lucrative tourist attraction, part of a disappointing trend in the country for visiting enthusiasts, but a move which undoubtedly attracted much needed income to help boost the country's faltering economy.

Opposite page: The sole surviving 2-8-2 with MINAZ in the 21st century, and working until 2002, was powerful ALCO 1910 (W/No.66284 of 1925), formerly Cuban Railroad No.351. On 7 April 1998, it is climbing the last kilometre towards Ifrain Alfonso mill, Villa Clara Province, with a loaded train from the Pozo *acopio*. Steam survived here until 2005.

Right: The mill pilot at Pepito Tey, Cienfuegos Province, on 15 April 1998 was 2ft 6in gauge Baldwin 2-8-0 1236 (W/No.35459 of 1910), positioning loaded wagons at the *patio*. Regular steam working ended in 2002, upon closure of the mill.

Opposite page: A piglet risks becoming a meal sooner than bargained for, as Ifrain Alfonso's Baldwin 2-6-2 1635 (W/No.58556 of 1925) storms across the unprotected *autopista* crossing with a loaded train on 7 April 1998. This bridge, in Villa Clara Province, is one of several built over the 'Great Cuban Freeway' when financial support for infrastructural development was available from the Soviet Union. Such schemes faltered following the breakup of the Union. The white concrete bridges with unfished roads at least provided a means for prominently displaying distances to selected destinations along the freeway.

Below: On 8 April 1998, Baldwin 2-8-0 1426 (W/No.53282 of 1920) crosses the trestle bridge with a loaded train, on the approach to Marcelo Salado, Villa Clara Province. 'Inter-mill' workings continued until 2003, despite this mill having closed in 1999.

Above: Away from any obvious dirt roads and requiring serious off-road driving skills to reach this location on 8 April 1998, 2ft 3½in gauge Baldwin 2-8-0 1420 (W/No.53847 of 1920) has a full load from the Cambao *acopio*, heading through the lush countryside of Sancto Spiritus Province, en route to Obdulio Morales mill. Limited steam activity lasted here into the 2003 season.

On 9 April 1998, ALCO 2-8-0 1837 (W/No.62543 of 1920) was busily engaged in positioning loaded cane wagons at Orlando Gonzalez Ramirez mill, Ciego de Avilla Province. Intensive steam activity, using four locos, continued here until 2002, including the use of a rare ALCO 4-6-0. Upon the influx of diesel traction by the 2003 *zafra*, the mill retained steam in reserve to diesel traction for two further years.

During the early evening of 9 April 1998, Vulcan Ironworks 2-6-0 1564 (W/No.2449 of 1916) was shunting the arrival sidings at Ecuador mill, Ciego de Avila Province. During the 2003 and 2004 *zafra* seasons, most line work was in the hands of diesel locos, with limited duties remaining for steam, chiefly shunting at the *patio*, these lasting until the end of the 2004 season.

On 15 April 1998, Baldwin 2-8-0 1834 (W/No.52539 of 1919), originally Cuban Cane Sugar Co. No.100, prepares to move hopper wagons containing either refined sugar or molasses, to the F.C.C. exchange sidings at Ciro Redondo mill, Ciego de Avila Province. This was one of the last mills to regularly use steam traction. Shunting at the mill's extensive *patio* area ceased after the 2006 *zafra*, by which time steam-hauled tourist trains had become well established.

Above: On 10 April 1998, Baldwin 2-8-0 1388 (W/No.31375 of 1907), one of seven in the Rafael Freyre fleet of 2ft 6in gauge locos, blackens the rugged but lush countryside as it climbs away from the Uvilla *acopio*.

Right: Sister Baldwin 1386 (W/No.52630 of 1919) deposits empties in the siding near Barjay, with a rake of loaded cane wagons on the adjacent line, ready for collection and for transfer to the Santa Lucia mill on 13 April 1998.

On 13 April 1998, Rafael Freyre's Baldwin 2-8-0 1386 heads away from Barjay village with cane from Princesa *acopio* for Santa Lucia mill, traversing the reverse curves, and almost obliterating the renowned 'three hills' vista. The final *zafra* on this extensive, scenic, and much-loved system in Holguin Province, sadly proved to be 2002, by which time tourist trains had become well established, tapping into the market at the nearby popular tourist resort of Guardalavaca.

6

SOUTHERN AFRICA

The glory days of industrial steam on the African continent were all but over by the beginning of the 21st century, with just four locations where daily industrial steam could still be enjoyed on the 3ft 6in 'Cape Gauge'. In South Africa there were two locations, 600km apart. Both used ex-South African Railways (SAR) locos, the St. Helena gold mine near Allanridge in the Free State having a fleet of six 16CR Pacifics, and the Sappi Saiccor pulp mill at Umkomaas, near Durban, with three 19D Class 4-8-2s, the former with steam until 2002, and Sappi Saiccor using diesel from September 2015. Botswana and Zimbabwe thereafter flew the flag for regular steam operations. The immediate future of the 100% steam-worked railway in Botswana, using four ex-National Railways of Zimbabwe (NRZ) and SAR main line locos, two of which were used daily at the Selebi Phikwe copper mine of Bamangwato Concessions Ltd (BCL), seemed assured in 2015, especially with the low prices its copper and nickel products were attracting, thereby reducing the likelihood of investment in diesel traction. Sadly, BCL's commercial standing deteriorated to such a degree that it suddenly terminated its production on 7 October 2016. It was unsurprising that financially depressed Zimbabwe, with its own coal reserves at Hwange, would continue using steam traction, with it possibly outliving steam on systems elsewhere in the world. 'Garratt' locos had either been purchased from the NRZ, or latterly hired-in and supplied on a rotational basis from the NRZ depot at Bulawayo. But availability of spares for steam was proving increasingly problematic and diesels took over during late 2018, seemingly marking the end of regular working industrial steam on the African continent. Steam had been retained in reserve, and was used again briefly in July 2019, when diesel fuel was too expensive, so this may not yet be the end of the story!

Timber traffic is the mainstay on Sappi Saiccor's railway at Umkomaas in South Africa's Natal south coast region. Additionally, two weekly coal consignments arrive for the plant. Steam usually worked ten-wagon rakes up to the plant. On 6 June 2015, after moving the first ten wagons of coal, 19D Class 4-8-2 No.2 (ex-SAR 2633) had returned to the exchange yard for the remainder, and made a spirited departure. Directly behind the vacuum-fitted loco's tender is an air brake compressor wagon to provide compatibility with the modern air-braked timber wagons. The large silver pipe dominating the railway's course carries non-toxic waste from the plant. Umkomaas pulp mill has two claims to fame; it is the world's largest producer of chemical cellulose, and was the last user of commercial industrial steam in South Africa. (Warwick Falconer)

With the tide out and a storm brewing over the sea, No.2 puts on an impressive display hauling wagons of eucalyptus pulp wood bound for Sappi Saiccor's processing plant, 1km upstream in the Umkomaas river valley. The Natal coast in South Africa has a tropical climate and, even though this was mid-winter on 6 June 2015, any exhaust effect was negligible at 30C plus, unless the loco was being fired. (Warwick Falconer)

Above left: On 5 June 2015, 19D Class 4-8-2s No.3 (ex-SAR 2797), and in steam behind, No.2 (SAR 2633), were the only remaining serviceable engines, with diesel traction replacing them permanently in September 2015.

Above right: On 12 August 2000, during the last year of daylight workings at the mine, Class 16CR 4-6-2 No.6 (ex-SAR 817) propels empties from No.8 to No.10 shaft of the Gold Fields Ltd's St. Helena mines, near Welkom in the Free State.

Right: On 12 August 2000, 16CR No.2 (ex-SAR 819) rests outside the depot at St. Helena. The final night shift work for steam to No.10 shaft ended on 28 October 2002. Thereafter, SAR diesels served No.8 shaft directly over a new branch connecting with the main line. (All Warwick Falconer)

Left: Although 'real' steam working around the world in the 2010s was very thin on the ground, it clung on to life in Zimbabwe, where Hwange colliery continued to use steam in the shape of 15th/15A Class 4-6-4+4-6-4 'Garratts' purchased from the NRZ. On 7 June 2012, Hwange colliery No.11 (ex-NRZ 423) shunts at the south end of the colliery/coking plant complex. (Richard Stevens)

Opposite page: On 7 June 2012, No.11 shunts in the depths of the colliery/ coking plant complex. (Richard Stevens)

Right: On 7 June 2012, No.11 pauses in the heart of the Hwange colliery/ coking plant complex. It failed during the following morning, and although it was repaired it eventually became a terminal failure. However, steam continued to perform for several more years, using hired-in 'Garratts' from NRZ, all four of the surviving in-traffic NRZ locos seeing use. By late 2018, however, NRZ was sending a diesel loco from Thomson Junction to work the colliery as required, and yet another country had lost its regular steam working. (Richard Stevens)

Left: BCL's Selebi shaft in Botswana provided its copper smelter with five out of the six loads required daily, the remaining load originating in the early morning from a shaft to the north of the plant. The usual 20-wagon train lengths on the system weighed in at around 1,360 tons. On 10 June 2015, 19D Class No.806 edges forward as its wagons are gradually loaded at the Selebi shaft. Loaded trains ran down the grade with the transfers from either of the shafts to the main smelting plant. (Warwick Falconer)

Opposite page: On 11 June 2015, with the large Selebi Phikwe smelter complex as a prominent backdrop, 19D Class No.806 was in charge of a load of empty coal wagons for despatch to the exchange sidings with the Botswana national railway. (Warwick Falconer)

Right: BCL's fleet comprised mainly ex-South African 19D Class 4-8-2s, two of which were in steam each day for working ore and stores trains. On 10 June 2015, the smelter provided a pleasing industrial backdrop for an ex-NRZ 19th Class, No.804, running light within the main complex at Selebi Phikwe. (Warwick Falconer)

At monthly intervals, a loaded train visited the BCL Selebi Phikwe weighbridge located behind the smelter before despatch. On 26 April 2016, ex-NRZ 19th Class No.804 was engaged in this task. Sadly, BCL went into provisional liquidation at the beginning of October 2016, bringing an end to industrial steam working in Botswana, leaving Hwange colliery in Zimbabwe as the sole surviving industrial location in Southern Africa continuing to use steam. (Warwick Falconer)

7

INDIA

For much of the latter part of the twentieth century, India had been a favourite destination for experiencing steam activity, but the situation changed more rapidly in the final decade than most enthusiasts had expected, until by the new millennium, apart from the tourist mountain railways, just two regularly steam-worked industrial railways survived, at Tipong colliery in Assam in North East India bordering Myanmar (Burma), and at Riga sugar mill in Bihar state in East India bordering Nepal. Coal India Ltd at Tipong colliery acquired four surplus B Class 0-4-0 saddle tanks from the Darjeeling Himalayan Railway (DHR) in the late 1960s. Their 2ft gauge railway connected the drift mines with an unloading point about 2 miles down the valley, where coal was either transferred to road transport, or carried via an underground conveyor to the Indian Railways' metre-gauge exchange sidings. Regular industrial steam ended at this extreme outpost of India in 2008, replaced by diesel. The former DHR saddle tanks, latterly augmented by the last working William Bagnall 0-4-0 saddle tank from the nearby Ledo brickworks, were retained, and have since been steamed for visiting enthusiasts.

Riga sugar mill, near Sitamarhi, had the distinction of operating the last commercial industrial steam loco to regularly work in India, just outstripping Tipong colliery. It is one of the oldest established sugar mills in the country, originally commencing production in 1933 under British management. As well as using rail transport, a significant quantity of cane was also brought into the mill from the surrounding fields using ox carts. Despite the use of traditional methods of transport, the Riga Sugar Company Ltd's (RSCL) mill is state-of-the-art, totally rebuilt between 1999 and 2000, and owned by the successful Bihar-based Dhanuka Group. It produces sugar, molasses, ethanol, and organic fertilisers. The anachronistic steam-worked metre-gauge railway serving the modern mill was dismantled after the winter 2008/09 season, when the Indian Railways' metre-gauge Darbhanga - Narkatiaganj line was converted to broad gauge, forcing the use of more modern methods of rail transport, and steam's redundancy. The photos in this chapter, at both Riga and Tipong, are of happier times in the late 20th century, although the final full year of regular steam working at both locations proved to be 2008.

On 22 December 1992, former DHR No.789 is seen from across the river valley, soon after leaving Tipong colliery. Unlike the other two locos in use on this date, Nos.784 and 796, sister loco No.789 was facing downhill away from the colliery. (David Moulden – Richard Stevens collection)

Left: On 22 December 1992, No.789 was busy shunting tubs containing pit props and other mining materials at Tipong, with the photographer being diligently observed by two security guards. Due to unrest in this border region, and the threat of potential abduction, all visitors to the colliery were 'shadowed' by security guards. (David Moulden – Richard Stevens collection)

Opposite page: On 21 December 1992, No.784 leaves the neck of the drift mine sidings whilst shunting a rake of nineteen partly loaded tubs. (David Moulden – Richard Stevens collection)

Right: Riga sugar mill's metre-gauge 1930-built Hudswell Clarke 0-8-0 saddle tank (W/No.1644) was a remarkable survivor in India, well into the 21st century. Due to unrest in this border region, the colliery security guards were armed and made regular patrols, especially when foreign visitors were present, as will be noted in this photograph. This Leeds-built loco of classic Hudswell Clarke design worked its last seasonal sugar cane traffic during the 2008/09 season, just before the main line serving the mill had been converted to broad gauge.

Left: Watched by many out-of-work local inhabitants on a cold 11 January 1999, after transferring laden cane wagons brought in from the exchange sidings, Riga's eight-coupled Hudswell Clarke busies itself positioning them into the sugar mill yard.

Opposite page: A typically chaotic and timeless scene at Riga mill's reception sidings, as both rail and ox cart transport compete for attention at the cane reception point. The standby 1935-built four-wheel diesel-mechanical behind the loaded cane wagon, yet another Leeds-built product, was happily a non-runner during this visit on 11 January 1999.

Right: Having just collected a rake of loaded cane wagons from the exchange sidings on 11 January 1999, the anonymous Hudswell Clarke loco has split its inbound load and is in the process of shunting them into the mill reception yard, under the watchful eye of alternative transport competition, patiently waiting to be called forward to deposit their harvested cane, but many hours of waiting would be in prospect for them, with rail traffic afforded priority.

8

MYANMAR (BURMA)

Above: During an organised group visit and photographic charter in February 2006, William Bagnall 2-6-2 No.42 (W/No.2338 of 1928) is shunting ore wagons in Namtu yard, with the Kerr Stuart 'Huxley' Class 0-4-2 tank No.13 (W/No.2383 of 1914), also in steam, standing by alongside. (John Sloane)

Left: Kerr Stuart 0-4-2 tank No.13 stands at the Wallah Gorge loading bunkers, with four ore wagons being loaded, each hopper wagon containing 20 tons of graded ore destined for Namtu smelter. (John Sloane)

The Burma Mines Railway & Smelting Co. at Namtu, in the north east of Shan State, was founded in 1906, to transport lead recovered from centuries-old waste tips of former silver workings dating from the period of Chinese influence. Until 1911, the recovered ore was taken over the 225km journey to Mandalay for smelting. This recovery process developed into renewed mining for silver, lead, and cobalt, requiring a more extensive railway for a new smelter built at Namtu. By 1929, a total of forty-seven 2ft gauge steam locos, principally of British manufacture from Kerr Stuart, but also ten William Bagnall 2-6-2 tender engines, had been acquired for the 70km system between the main line at Namyao, the smelter at Namtu, and mines around Bawdwin. During the 1930s slump, around a third of the older locos were taken out of service. Ten new Orenstein & Koppel (O&K) diesels were procured in 1979, and these have since worked 'main line' ore trains over the 11km section between Wallah Gorge and Namtu. Main line steam work ended soon after their arrival, but limited shunting was still undertaken thereafter by the last two operational steam locos. Until 1999, William Bagnall 2-6-2 No.42 (W/No.2338 of 1928) worked the Myanmar Railways exchange yard at Namyao, 50km from Namtu. The Kerr Stuart 'Huxley' Class 0-4-2 tank No.13 (W/No.2383 of 1914) and No.42 are believed to have seen further use around Namtu yard until around 2002. Upon their 'semi-retirement', these two veterans were retained for photographic charters. The original smelter at Namtu was destroyed during the 2nd World War, and its replacement structure has not been used since 2000. It had received ore from the remote Bawdwin deep mines, and use of steam on this section of line down to Wallah Gorge, where ore is graded and fed into loading bunkers, is understood to have ceased in 1988. The new smelting facility at Namtu, built to replace the sixty-year-old structure, is supplied with ore mined at Tiger Camp, near Wallah Gorge. The 8km mountain section of line between the Bawdwin mines and Wallah Gorge now sees only occasional freight traffic by rail, and the line between Namtu and the main line at Namyao fell into disuse in 2006. Outgoing product comprising lead, zinc, silver, and gold, was subsequently conveyed by road. Loaded trains were last handled by steam traction on this section of the railway in 1984.

Above: Kerr Stuart 0-4-2 tank No.13 is engaged in shunting a line of mixed rolling stock in Namtu yard.

Right: No.42 crosses the girder river bridge at Namtu with a demonstration freight. (Both John Sloane)

9

INDONESIA – JAVA

Java was the last stronghold in the world for industrial steam on the narrow gauge, possessing a variety of German, Dutch and Belgian locos working during the sugar cane harvest, usually between June and September. Following Cuba's rapid demise of steam early in the 21st century, Java became a favourite destination for industrial steam, next to China, but that is not to imply that steam's decline had not already gathered momentum, due to the falling price of sugar on world markets. By the new millennium, many mills had already been rationalised and converted to road transport, or had obtained diesel locos, and only the larger and more efficient mills survived. Nevertheless, a visit to the island in 2004 found fourteen mills using steam traction, albeit some working alongside diesels, with around fifty steam locos employed on four different gauges, many having seen over seventy-five years of service. These were mainly built by Orenstein & Koppel (O&K), but products from other manufacturers were also evident, including those from Berliner Maschinenfabrik A.G. (BMAG), Couillet, Du Croo & Brauns (D&B), Hartmann, Henschel, Jung, Krauss, and Maffei. Sadly, by this time most locos were engaged in simply moving cane wagons (*loris*) over short distances between the mills' reception points and their co-located road delivery points. In most cases this appeared to make the rail operations superfluous, but some crushing plants were still configured for deliveries entirely by rail. Notable exceptions were at Olean and Asembagus mills, both in East Java, where the rail solution into the fields continued, steam traction transporting cut cane directly from the distant field loading points, with buffalos hauling *loris* along lighter transportable tracks between the field cutting sites and the permanent trackway. Locos in Java burned chiefly bagasse fuel; the waste product created from cane crushing prior to its rendering process. The resultant waste was subsequently dried and compressed, the bales used as a free source of fuel for mill furnaces and locos alike, but large volumes were required, so many locos towed auxiliary tenders.

Opposite page: On 4 August 2004, fire quickly chases through the bare cane fields outside Sindanglaut mill. The stubble was incinerated to produce fertile ash for the subsequent year's harvest. D&B 720mm gauge 0-8-0 tank 8 (W/No.25 of 1924), in its last year of service, is silhouetted against the fire, the smoke from the advancing blaze partially covering the mill and adding to the pollution.

Right: On 13 August 2004, 700mm gauge O&K 0-4-2 tank 4 (W/No.893 of 1901), and 0-8-0 tank 8 (W/No.11348 of 1927), produce their signature sparks from the bagasse, as they work *loris* into Merican mill.

Above: The loco shed of the 600mm gauge system at Pangka mill, south of Tegal, at lunchtime on 5 August 2004 – on the left is spare loco, Jung 0-6-2 tender/tank 1 (W/No.2294 of 1915), and alongside and in steam is O&K 0-8-0 tender tank 10 (W/No.12457 of 1933). The stacked wood in the foreground and in the tenders suggests that these locos were predominately burning wood, rather than the more usual bagasse fuel. Regular steam activity remained until the end of the 2014 season.

Left: On 5 August 2004, standing around the turntable of this remarkably grand and ornate semi-roundhouse at Jatibarang mill in north central Java, south of Tegal, were Couillet 0-6-0 tank 1 (W/No.1572 of 1910) waiting for a boiler wash-out, and Jung 0-8-0 tank 5 (W/No.2387 of 1916) in steam. Regular steam working ceased on this 600mm gauge system by 2009, replaced by Japanese diesels.

Inside the loco shed at Sumberharjo mill, near Pemalang city, during the morning of 6 August 2004, were 700mm gauge *(left to right)* D&B 0-8-0 tank 9 (W/No.81 of 1925), O&K 0-8-0 tank 7 (W/No.11804 of 1929), O&K 0-8-0 tank 3 (W/No.5857 of 1912), D&B 0-8-0 tank 10 (W/No.29 of 1924) and D&B 0-8-0 tank 6 (W/No.12 of 1923). Sumberharjo was to be the last in Java to use steam for hauling cane from the fields to the mill, mainly at night, until the end of the 2011 season, with up to five locos in use each day for this work, plus two deployed for mill shunting. Regular use of steam at the mill ended at the close of the 2014 season.

Left: On 6 August 2004, 700mm gauge D&B 0-8-0 tank 10 (W/No.29 of 1924), with an auxiliary tender for the bagasse fuel, positions laden *loris*, brought in overnight to the cane reception yard at Sumberharjo mill, near Pemalang in Tegal region, as a group of schoolchildren make their way home through the busy mill yard, clearly as a matter of daily routine.

Right: Locos in Java, although primarily fuelled by bagasse, also burned wood if there was a supply. On 7 August 2004, 600mm gauge BMAG 0-10-0 tank *Sragi VII* (W/No.9318 of 1928) is replenished with wood for lighting up purposes, following attention at the maintenance shed at Sragi mill. A remarkable steam fleet from nine different manufacturers had been used to bring cane in from the fields until 2003, and continued to work the short transfers until the end of the 2014 season.

Opposite page: On 9 August 2004, 750mm gauge O&K 0-8-0 tender tank 5 (WNo.9513 of 1921) with loaded *loris* heads away from the cane loading point along the 'street running' section between residential properties and towards Tasikmadu mill. Two labourers are perched on the front of the loco taking refuge from the sun beneath a makeshift corrugated tin shade, diligently applying sand to the rails. This was a scene that had been, and continued to be played out over many years.

Left: On 9 August 2004, 750mm gauge O&K 0-8-0 tender tank 5 (W/No.9513 of 1921) was employed on shunting duties at the Tasikmadu mill, located east of Solo.

Opposite page: On 11 August 2004, O&K 700mm gauge jackshaft gear-driven 0-8-0 tank 10 *Salak* (W/No.8090 of 1910), the last working example of its kind in the country, but by this time held in reserve to a diesel, and here working by special arrangement, draws a loaded cane train through the yard at Rejosari mill, south west of Madiun. Daily steam working continued until 2003, after which two locos were held in reserve to diesels until the 2012 season.

Right: A visit to the Tasikmadu mill's loco shed at staff break on 8 August 2002, found massive 750mm gauge O&K 'Luttermöller' 0-10-0 *VI* (W/No.11790 of 1929) ready to assume line work duties. Although classified as a 'Decapod', its leading and end driving wheels do not have connecting rods to the centre drivers, instead power is transmitted by an ingenious geared system, allowing these articulated locos to negotiate sharp curves. Alongside, but not in steam was Henschel 0-8-0 tender tank *7B* (W/No.11917 of 1913). By August 2015, regular steam operations at Tasikmadu had ceased, with steam subsequently used only on tourist and charter operations.

Above left: Kanigoro mill, just south of Madiun on 12 August 2004, with 700mm gauge O&K 0-8-0 tank 6 (W/No.9447 of 1921) on a loaded train at the mill reception sidings. Steam finally ended here after the 2015 season.

Above right: A hot and humid day at Purwodadi mill, near the city of Ngawi, on 11 August 2004, finds 700mm gauge O&K 0-8-0 tank 16 (W/No.4359 of 1910) positioning loaded *loris*. Up to four steam locos continued to find use until the end of the 2019 season, the last mill in Java to use conventional steam.

Right: Pagottan mill, south of Madiun, on 12 August 2004 with O&K 0-10-0 tank 6 (W/No.10606 of 1923) trundling through the yard. This 700mm gauge 'Luttermöller', and its two sister locos were converted to fireless operation from the 2011 season, and all were still at work minus their tenders during the 2021 harvest, the last surviving steam-powered locos working in industry in Java.

700mm gauge O&K 0-4-2 tank 4 (W/No.893 of 1901), by then the oldest working loco in Java, pauses between shunting duties at Merican mill's loading point on 12 August 2004, allowing traditional animal power to take priority. It was out of use by 2010, but steam continued in use at this Kediri region mill into 2011.

The procession just prior to sunset of several loaded trains from the cane fields to Olean mill was a daily spectacle for locals and visiting enthusiasts alike during the harvesting season in these traditional villages of East Java. On 14 August 2004, 700mm gauge O&K 5 *Bromo* (W/No.9358 of 1920) stirs up the dust with its long trailing load on the Semering branch line, picking it sinuous route through the village streets, seen here approaching the triangle between the villages of Tribungen and Karang Malang. Steam's field work swan song at Olean proved to be during the 2008 season, thereafter being confined to mill work until 2014, or occasional chartered trains from the cane fields.

With fish laid out to dry in the sun, and a police motorcyclist observing the proceedings, Asembagus mill's 700mm gauge O&K 0-6-0 tank 11 (W/No.9459 of 1920) crosses the Situbondo road and enters Jangkou harbour gates, with a specially arranged box van train on 14 August 2004. The all-pervading aroma in the vicinity was distinctly pungent in the hot midday sun! Steam continued to find sporadic field work at Asembagus into 2010.

Left: Early morning at Semboro on 15 August 2004, with 700mm gauge O&K 0-6-0 fireless 3 (W/No.11927 of 1929) in action. By this time it was one of an identical pair employed on ash removal work, using a short section of line at the mill, and seeing employment until the end of the 2018 season.

Right: Cane cutters are returning home just before sunset on 15 August 2004, as 700mm gauge Jung 0-6-0 tank 29 (W/No.13490 of 1961) returns its trailing load of cane to Semboro mill. By this time held in reserve to diesel traction, the 1961-built 'youngster' (in comparison to most other steam locos in Java) was put into action for a visiting party, following a trend previously established in Cuba, and predictably perpetuated in Java as the number of active steam locos in industry declined.

The Mount Argopuro volcano (3,088m) in East Java is visible through the heat haze in the right background on 15 August 2004 as, by special arrangement, 700mm gauge O&K 'Mallet' 0-4-4-0 tank 15 (W/No.11262 of 1926) heads a mixed rake of wagons from the Semboro mill into the fields. The 'V' skips contained waste ash from the sugar refining process, used for fertilising the fields.

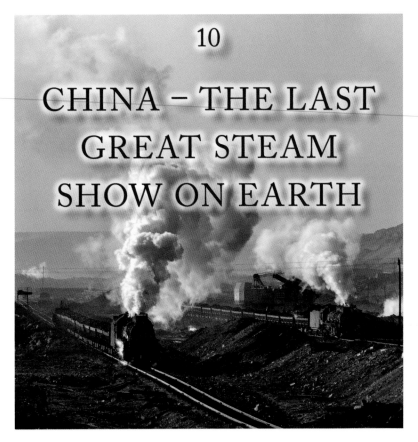

10

CHINA – THE LAST GREAT STEAM SHOW ON EARTH

By the end of steam's demise on the China National Railway (CNR) in 2003, and after the QJ Class 2-10-2s had turned their wheels for the last time on the provincial JiTong Railway in Inner Mongolia in 2005, there was already a keen interest being shown in the surviving industrial systems in China, which were still using steam in large numbers. A handful of industrial systems even bore a resemblance to former CNR steam operations, especially those using QJ and JS mixed traffic locos on timetabled passenger services alongside their principal coal traffic. Prime examples were the railways serving the 'coal cities' of Shuangyashan in the far north east, and Pingdingshan in central China. The Chinese government had a vision of eradicating steam by 2008, the occasion of the Beijing Olympic Games, but this proved to be impracticable. The country continued to be the 'number one' location in the world for seeing steam in its raw and often harsh industrial environment, generally far away from the accepted tourist trails. Although surviving industrial steam on offer by the 21st century lacked variety in class, this was amply compensated by the varied environments in which they operated. The comparative ease of access to the industrial complexes and railways further made visits a rewarding prospect. Industrial steam classes surviving were the QJ Class 2-10-2, and JS Class 2-8-2, both of 1950s design and having seen widespread use on the CNR, but with some examples of both classes being delivered directly to industry. Use of the PL2 Class 2-6-2 of a 1935 Japanese design for light steelworks duties, was all but over, however the standard industrial mixed traffic industrial loco, the SY Class 2-8-2, built in large numbers between 1960 and 1999, found widespread deployment. The final SY Class member to see regular use on any colliery system was notably to be found in the Mongolian Autonomous Region, working until as recently as September 2021, although unusually, one class member was converted to run on compressed air, and was last seen active in November 2018 at a Tianjin engineering works in Hebei Province. Central China proved to be the final stamping ground of the mighty QJ 2-10-2, the last working examples, built specifically for industrial service in a batch at Datong works in the late 1980s, remained in use at Zoucheng, in Shandong Province, until March 2011. However, it is the JS 'Mikado' that will finally bring the curtain down on Chinese industrial steam, at the Sandaoling mines in Xinjiang Province. This event is imminent as the year 2022 unfolds, its fleet of up to ten JS in daily use already having been threatened on two previous occasions.

Left: At dawn on 9 January 2016, coal scavengers wait patiently to resume sifting through waste progressively dumped into the worked-out opencast mine at Fuxin in a futile attempt to fill the massive chasm created over many years of coal extraction. SY 1320 from Wulong mine sits at the head of its rake of tippler wagons being systematically discharged. Wulong mine was suddenly closed seven months later, a devastating blow to Fuxin, bringing an end to steam traction in this modern sprawling city in the north west of Liaoning Province. Also known as the 'Agate City', around half of China's known deposits of this mineral are to be found there, whilst its coal reserves have significantly dwindled in recent decades from over-exploitation.

Opposite page: On 16 January 2016, JS 8167 heaves its load away from the Sandaoling opencast loading point, as sister JS 8197 is being prepared by its crew to follow in its tracks as soon as the section is clear. This daily steam-worked system was the last commercial industrial operation in the world to regularly employ steam traction on such a large scale.

Right: In the indescribably freezing conditions of 2 January 2001, around -40C, when even the resilient city dwellers found it a challenge to keep warm, QJ 7019 makes its presence known upon its departure from the CNR exchange sidings, during the final months of steam at Shuangyashan. The two sure-footed ladies managed to beat the moving train without incident, understandably not wishing to stand around unnecessarily.

On a warm 28 September 2003, C2 No.1 of the Dahuichang Limestone Railway rattles along the 2km double-track running line with its rake of four-wheel tubs, approaching the quarry loading point. The cement works, where the limestone would be deposited using the rotary tippler, and subsequently crushed and processed, is visible to the top left. This charming railway transported its last stone in July 2005. The ubiquitous Chinese 762mm gauge C2 Class 0-8-0, based on a Russian design and built in large numbers in China between 1958 and 1988, saw widespread use in the country on coal, aggregates, and timber lines, and even on passenger trains.

The 762mm gauge Dahuichang Limestone Railway, located on the south western fringes of Beijing was an accessible and compact railway to visit, often at the start of a tour taking in some more distant provinces. On 28 December 2002, a day when loaded stone trains were running at 15-minute intervals, C2 No.1 is leaving the discharge and crushing plant area with the final rake of empties for loading that day, just before sunset. This chapter on China is presented in something like a geographical sequence, commencing in the central and southern regions, moving down as far as Sichuan Province, returning to Henan and Hebei Provinces, before crossing via south west Inner Mongolia to the north west provinces of Gansu and Xinjiang, and back across to the extreme north east Heilongjiang Province, on the way taking in some locations in Liaoning Province, and finally visiting the northern area of the Mongolian Autonomous Region.

South, Central, and West China

Central and southern China was a rich hunting ground for industrial steam, but was particularly challenging for photography, due to its warm and wet climatic conditions, certainly compared to those harsh winter months prevailing in the north east of the country, where dramatic steam action photography was more readily achievable. The Uygur Autonomous Region, widely covered in recent media reports, has attracted attention from steam enthusiasts for its surviving steam-worked operations at Sandaoling, the last anywhere in the world on such a scale. During 2011, and not so widely recognised, the QJ was to see out its final days in the central region of China, long after their demise on CNR, and six years after their withdrawal from service on the provincial JiTong Railway. The Pingdingshan Coal Administration's railway, in Henan Province, around 830km south west of Beijing, was unique in the 21st century because all three of the main industrial classes worked there. Their QJ, JS, and SYs (a fleet of 6, 13, and 10 respectively in 2003) were employed on coal trains around this extensive system, with the 'Mikados' entrusted to its passenger services, running approximately 25km north east to No.13 Mine, and about 50km north west to Baofeng and Gaozhuangzhan.

Opposite page: On a heavily overcast and polluted day, 8 January 2003, JS 6253 tackles the steep ascent from Pingdingshan city with empties for No.4 Mine, passing a small-scale private mining enterprise. This branch on the north western fringe of the city served Nos.2, 4, and 6 Mines. The Pingdingshan region, developed from around 1957 and built upon high quality coal reserves, possessed over 35 productive coal mines, of which 13 were served by this railway in 2003. The city derives its name from the long, flat mountain to the north east, by which it is overlooked.

Right: Further down into Pingdingshan city on the same day, QJ 2035, originally with CNR Lanzhou Bureau, has arrived at No.2 Mine and commences positioning the empty wagons into the mine's loading point, before collecting the fulls. Just seconds after this event, a couple frantically emerged from their rudimentary dwelling to the right and hurriedly gathered up their washing from the line tethered between the signal and water column! By early 2003, the number of QJs found in industrial and local railway service was rapidly dwindling, with most of the remaining active class members at that time working on the provincial JiTong Railway, where they understandably commanded much greater attention. No longer a main line runner, the smoke deflectors had been unceremoniously removed from this veteran Datong 1974-built QJ to improve the crew's sight lines when shunting yards and sidings.

Above: Alongside Pingdingshan coking plant at sunrise on 8 January 2003, Tangshan 1975-built SY 1002 was on yard pilot duties, propelling wagons into the extensive Tianzhuang holding sidings from the headshunt at the east end of the yard.

Below: On 2 January 2003, Datong 1987-built JS 8122 is at the head of train 104, the 10:10 service from Gaozhuangzhan to Pingdingshan Zhongxin, making its first call, adjacent to Gaozhuang mine, on this westernmost section of the extensive Pingdingshan Mines railway system. Basic passenger accommodation, filthy both inside and out, was provided in the late 1980s-built YZ22 coaches. Many passengers sat on newspapers or plastic bags to protect their clothes, and the external metal grilles fitted over the soot-encrusted and brake-dust-stained windows made vision through them almost impossible. Main access to the platform at Gaozhuangzhan was achieved by stepping across two steel hawsers engaged in drawing wagons through the mine's coal loader!

Left: On a cold and smoggy late morning, 8 January 2003, ex-works QJ 6450, built at Datong works in 1983, lifts a long rake of empties out of Tianzhuang yard, as Datong 1988-built JS 8338 busies itself making up a train for a subsequent departure to an outlying mine on the extensive Pingdingshan Mining Railway system.

Right: Vigilantly observed by a female crossing keeper around midday on 31 December 2002, Tangshan 1990-built SY 1687 storms out of the murk of Shenxi Yard, crossing a minor road in the crowded suburbs of the tightly packed basic uniform housing of Pingdingshan. The long rake of empties will have originated from the city's power plant, destined for reloading at No.2 Mine.

Opposite page: Viewed from a pagoda on a disused slag tip at sunset in the polluted city of Pingdingshan on 10 January 2003, JS 8057 steadily slogs up the branch to No.4 Mine with empties for loading. No.2 Mine, with its slag tip and pagoda prominent to the right, can be seen beyond the rear of this train, and the city's power plant is to the top left. A generating station surrounded by city residential housing is not an uncommon sight in China, such key facilities are all too soon proved inadequate as the populations of the cities grow exponentially.

Above right: On 30 December 2002, QJ 7186, tackles the steep ascent into Tianzhuang Yard from Pingdingshan Dong CNR exchange sidings. A trailing load of 67 empty 'gondola' wagons was a relatively easy task for this mighty Datong works-built locomotive, one of the final class members built, and delivered directly into industrial service in 1987. The QJ was designed primarily for CNR service, and was the most numerous class of steam loco in China, numbering 4,700 since their first introduction in 1956. A final batch of around 25 QJs was built specifically for industrial service before steam production ended at the Datong works in late 1988. QJ 7186 and a handful of other class members, found in various industrial locations in south central China, served for the entire two decades of service or more expected of them. Unsurprisingly, QJ 7186 continued working until the cessation of regular steam working at Pingdingshan during summer 2008, and its sisters 7189 and 7190 with the Yanzhou Coal Mining Bureau at Zoucheng, in Shandong Province, finally bowed out in March 2011.

Below right: On 6 January 2003, the sun attempts to pierce the murk around No.8 Mine on the Pingdingshan system, as pilot loco Datong 1983-built JS 6253 vigorously shunts the sidings. A signal and telecommunications gang move their equipment on a trolley out of the way from the main running line alongside the mine, as Datong 1984-built QJ 6786, with a load from Yuzhou mine, waits for a clear road ahead to proceed to Pingdingshan Dong CNR exchange sidings. The main running lines on this system were substantially laid, and much work was in progress updating the colour light signalling along this section of line. There were three independent QJs based at Yuzhou, specifically for moving heavy coal trains to Pingdingshan Dong from the Yuzhou mines. Although not the responsibility of the Pingdingshan Coal Administration, they were maintained at the main depot at Pingdingshan and used its metals between Pingdingshan, No.8 Mine, and Renshiguang, where the lines split for No.13 Mine and Yuzhou.

Left: On 9 October 2003, in typically overcast conditions for the Sichuan region, 762mm gauge C2 No.32 returns empties to Huangjianggou mine, crossing an impressive, curved viaduct. The 6km line from Huangjianggou to Nihe, built in 1958, was operated on behalf of the Weiyuan Coal Company, and moved coal to a power plant and cement works at Nihe. The railway company owned a fleet of six Class C2s and had operated a passenger service up until 1988. At the time of this visit there were just the two operational locos, neither in the best of health. The railway struggled on until 2007, finally succumbing to road dumper trucks.

Opposite page: On 9 October 2003, a decrepit No.32 stands at the colliery loading chutes in heavily polluted Huangjianggou, as its wagons are slowly loaded with coal destined for Nihe power plant.

Right: On 3 October 2004, C2 No.32 leaves the Nihe power plant's compound with empty wagons for reloading at Huangjianggou colliery loading point.

Shibanxi, in Sichuan Province, is about 100km south of Chengdu, and home to a 20km long 762mm gauge railway, built in 1958. On 8 October 2003, C2 No.7 pauses at Sanjin as passengers disembark and head for home with their day's purchases. Administered by the Jiayang Power Company, the line was electrified from Shibanxi to Sanjin mine, with steam locos working passenger and coal trains throughout between Shibanxi, Bagou and Huangcunjin. The local passenger service was withdrawn in August 2021, but steam-hauled passenger services remain on this scenic railway, which has now been transformed into one catering entirely for tourist coach parties.

The Huangcunjin drift mine, with its 300mm gauge hand-worked line, adjoined the 762mm gauge Shibanxi Railway. On 7 October 2003, a miner takes a well-earned rest as he waits for the labourers to move away from the coal tipping area, before tipping his precious and freshly hewn consignment of high quality coal. C2 No.14 is busying itself below making up its loaded train for transfer down the valley to Shibanxi. This traffic from the drift mines at the head of the valley ended by summer 2012. Freight on the railway had been chiefly coal and limited timber traffic downhill, with bricks and aggregates for building work around Bagou occasionally conveyed uphill.

A remarkable survivor well into the 21st century was the 762mm gauge clay railway serving Xingyang brickworks, in Henan Province, 25km west of Zhengzhou city, exploiting the rich clay deposits just south of the Yellow River. On an extremely wet 30 September 2003, when quarry operations were to be imminently suspended in the persistently heavy rainfall, C2 No.207 had a full load of clay, in a rake of twenty-six side-tipping wagons, and would shortly trundle away from the rudimentary loading point and on to the run-down brickworks in a bucolic setting, located some 5km distant, running over a terrain of worked-out excavations, deep cuttings, and a tall five-arch viaduct, crossing well stocked fishponds. The sporadic operations on this railway, influenced by the weather conditions, are thought to have ended around March 2011, shortly after a tragic head-on collision occurred along the railway.

A brown dust from the thriving works of the Handan Iron and Steel Company settles on all the surrounding city buildings in Handan, in Hebei Province. On 13 January 2003, SY 1658, with its barrier wagon and ladles, draws away from the blast furnaces with a heavy load of molten slag. The works used a fleet of fourteen 'Mikados' at this time, working alongside a small number of diesels which were just beginning to infiltrate. Further arrivals eventually eradicated all steam working by the end of 2006.

Baotou Steelworks, Inner Mongolia, on 15 January 2001, with 1972-built SY 0501 working a rake of slag ladles. The works dominates the western part of the city and at this time employed a fleet of over twenty mainly Tangshan-built SYs, which were entirely displaced by diesel traction from January 2009. (Don White)

On 25 November 2005, the morning sun makes a futile attempt to penetrate the pollution, as Tangshan 1971-built SY 0362 clanks across the Datong River bridge near Haishiwan, Gansu Province, with alumina from the CNR exchange sidings bound for Yaojie. The SYs also conveyed coal from two Yaojie area mines to Haishiwan along the 12km branch, and seven SYs remained in the Yaojie Coal Railway's fleet at this time, but within a year it was dieselised. The precipitous access path perched precariously high above the deep river valley was covered with sheet ice, enabling a slippery arrival on the photographic spot far quicker than expected, and just in the nick of time! The bridges beyond the railway carry the main highway and the Lanzhou–Xining CNR line.

On 2 December 2005, high up in the valley, 7km from the 'copper city' of Baiyin, in Gansu Province, the lead/zinc smelter of the Baiyin Non-Ferrous Metals Company at Sanyelian is in full production and polluting the valley as Tangshan 1975-built SY 1047 noisily slogs up the grade with empty ore tippler wagons destined for loading at the Kuangsan copper mines at Shenbutong, some 19km from Baiyin Shi. Diesel traction first arrived during 2010, but limited steam activity continued until 2017.

Against all expectations, steam traction continued to serve the Sandaoling opencast mine, 60km west of Hami in Xinjiang Province, the officially designated Uygur Autonomous Region, until 2022. On 16 January 2016, the fireman has been piling on the coal as Datong works 1987-built JS 8081 makes its final assault out of the opencast mine at Kengkouzhan heading for Xibolizhan yard, with the snow-capped peaks of the Tianshan mountain range at 4,000m above sea level clearly dominating the background scene on this clear, crisp morning. This was to be China's last outpost of steam traction on such a grand scale, and it was originally understood from local sources that Sandaoling would have retired its fleet of JS locos and abandoned rail traffic entirely in the opencast mine during 2017 in favour of road transport. After two postponements, the employment of steam in the opencast mine remarkably continued until early 2022. At the time of writing, a handful of JS Class 2-8-2s were still serving the two deep mines, accessed by the branch line from Nanzhan yard.

Above: Witnessing three trains simultaneously side by side in the opencast mine at Sandaoling called for good fortune, especially with the reduced output of the mine by 2016 compared to a decade previously, and this would usually only occur due to operational issues at the loading points. Such was the case on 20 January 2016, with JS 8225 and JS 8081 on the left awaiting access to the conveyor and bucket loaders respectively, and former CNR Lanzhou Bureau JS 8197 on the right, just leaving for Xibolizhan yard from the so-called 'Station 82' signal control point.

Opposite page: The remnants of snowfall from two days earlier have helped to lift this scene in the low afternoon light on 13 January 2016, as JS 8190 demonstrates its supreme strength in lifting a loaded train out of the opencast pit and on to either the Xuanmeichang washery, for stockpiling at Jianmeixian, or to the yard complex at Nanzhan for onward despatch via the CNR main line.

Above: Against the backdrop of the snow-capped peaks of the Tianshan Mountains, just visible through the mist and pollution on 17 January 2016, JS 8081 gets to grips with its rake of empty tippler wagons, heading away from the extensive coal discharge point at Jianmeixian. This stockpile, close to Nanzhan yard, contained coal primarily destined for the Hami District power station.

Opposite page: Photographing steam workings across the barren landscape between No.2 Mine and Nanzhan yard on the Sandaoling Coal Mines system could be a hit and miss affair, potentially involving hours of waiting around, and often proving to be fruitless. On 14 January 2016, former CNR Lanzhou Bureau JS 8358 has just arrived at No.2 Mine with CNR gondola wagons for loading, but would remain there for several hours.

Above left: On 29 November 2005, soon after fresh snowfall, and with the Tian Shan Mountains visible some 50km distant in the crystal-clear conditions of China's western desert region, Datong works 1987-built JS 8366 coasts down the grade through the freezing barren landscape with a loaded train from No.2 mine, with coal destined for Nanzhan yard and subsequently onward to the CNR system at Liushuguan exchange sidings. Following the cessation of steam working in the Sandaoling opencast pit, these unpredictable workings between Nanzhan yard and the two deep mines were still continuing in the hands of steam traction at the time of writing. The prevailing downhill grade for the infrequent loaded trains would make this an unattractive prospect for photographers considering a visit to this extremely sensitive region of China, and any foreign visitors could expect to be under surveillance frequently during their travels to and from Hami and around Sandaoling.

Below left: During the evening of 19 January 2016, the yard supervisor of Xuanmeichang discharge point, with his green lamp illuminated, walks ahead of an arrival from the Sandaoling opencast mine, the loaded train being gradually eased forward by the driver of Datong 1987-built JS 8225. Another JS 'Mikado' beyond is heading back to the mine for reloading, its rake of tippler wagons having just been discharged. Within the space of one hour, three loaded trains were handled at this washery location, which was often devoid of deliveries during daylight hours. A solitary bright yard lamp located behind the yard controller's hut offered an appreciable amount of illumination for the main approach area to these reception sidings.

Opposite page: The fires were thrown out of the remaining fleet of late 1980s-built JS 'Mikados' working in the opencast pit at Sandaoling in early 2022. As the sun weakens on the western horizon on 16 January 2016, JS 8081, built at Datong works in 1987, makes a sure-footed start away from the Xikeng loading point, fed by conveyor from the remaining dwindling workings in the pit. In the distance, sister JS 8225 positions its KF60 wagons alongside the electric shovel. This location was one in which it was not advisable to linger for too long, for whilst the ground was pleasantly warm underfoot in the freezing conditions, the sulphurous fumes emitting from voids in the smouldering ground, were to be avoided at all costs.

North East China

A busy early morning scene at Daqing on 22 November 1999, the principal servicing point on the Tiefa (aka Diaobingshan) Coal Mining Administration's railway system. SY 1769, completed at Tangshan works in June 1995, passes with loaded internal hopper wagons bound for the Tieling power plant. Several Tangshan 1990s-built classmates, with 1764 and 1751 visible in the foreground, are being prepared for their day's duties, with two officials present to scrutinise the visitors. This busy mining railway located 70km north of Shenyang City, in Liaoning Province, still boasted an intensive 100% steam-worked passenger service at the turn of the century. It had a network of around 60km of lines serving seven highly productive mines and two power plants, in the hands of a fleet of 18 SY 'Mikados', including the last standard-gauge steam loco built in China, in 1999. Despite this, diesel traction had already infiltrated by late 2003, and by 2008 steam had been eradicated from most freight traffic, although two of the newer SYs were retained for the passenger services on the Diaobingshan–Tieling and Diaobingshan–Faku lines until around 2010–11, thereafter being retained for special charter trains and annual public gala events.

Retained for specific duties in areas with restricted clearance within the steelworks at Anshan, in Liaoning Province, and Baotou, in Inner Mongolia, the PL2 Class 'Prairie' just survived into the 21st century, with the last active example seen working at Baotou in February 2002. On 19 March 1997, No.244 was in action deep inside the Anshan works in the vicinity of the blast furnaces, and was the last member of the class to remain in service there.

On 28 December 2004, Datong 1987-built JS 6243 of the Huludao Limestone Railway, one of four in the fleet for line work and supplemented by two SYs for shunting, heads a rake of heavy limestone and empty coal wagons at the Yangjiazhangzi works of the Liaoning Bohai Cement Group. Due to the heavy demand for cement in a burgeoning Chinese economy, steam saw extended use far beyond expectations on this 40km railway, but was finally ousted by diesel traction during 2010. (Don White)

The extensive Nanpiao Mining Railway was 40km west of Jinzhou, in the rolling hills typical of this region of Liaoning Province. On 11 January 2004, Tangshan 1993-built SY 1478, one of five working there at that time, draws empties away from Weizigou washery heading for Sanjiazi. This two-branch 35km system served various collieries and ran passenger services throughout. Various ex-CNR diesel classes were randomly acquired by the railway from late 2003, but limited steam working lingered on for seven more years, until its final extinction during early 2010. (Don White)

Above: The Yuanbaoshan Coal Railway, just over the border in Inner Mongolia, operated a small fleet of JS 'Mikados', working mixed trains to and from Fengshuigou colliery, and various trip and shunting duties on this compact railway system, which also connected with other mines and the CNR exchange sidings. On 16 November 2005, working hard on the steep ascent past the cement factory despite its modest trailing load, JS 6544 heads the early morning empties from Majiawan to the opencast mine. The system's limited steam activity finally ceased by late 2013.

Left: Early morning shift change at Zhuangmeizhan washery on the Pingzhuang Mining Railway, also just inside Inner Mongolia, on 19 November 2005, finds a gathering of SYs being serviced, prior to taking up their day's diagrams to the outlying deep mines and on track maintenance trains in the electrified opencast mine. SY 0400 is being steam-cleaned, whilst deflector-fitted SY 1083 stands on the ash disposal pit. Deflector-fitted SYs with the boiler top cowling behind the chimney were uncommon, significantly altering their overall appearance. Regular steam activity ended at Pingzhuang in 2017.

Left: Returning to Liaoning Province, during the last winter of steam action on the Fuxin Mining Railway, four 'Mikados' are being prepared for the evening shift on 9 January 2016. SYs 1359 and 1320 are at the front, with their safety valves lifting beneath the starlit sky at Wulong's Ping'an yard stabling point.

Right: On 11 January 2016, the Fuxin Mining Railway's Wulong area track-repair gang head out for their morning's routine PW maintenance work, as SY 1397, with spoil for disposal at the tip, draws away from Wulong colliery between the redundant electrification masts. During its final two years, steam primarily worked on mine rock waste disposal duties, coal to the power stations by then being in the hands of diesel traction, but the unexpected closure of Wulong mine in August 2016, after sixty years of winding coal, eliminated the use of steam traction.

On 11 January 2016, having deposited its mine waste, Fuxin Mining Railway's Tangshan 1987-built SY 1397 returns the empty tipplers to Wulong mine for reloading, climbing away along the former double-track electrified section once serving the 700m deep Haizhou opencast pit, which became worked-out by 2005. This area is gradually being returned to nature as the designated Haizhou Lutiankuang National Mine Park and Museum.

Fuxin Mining Railway's newly outshopped SY 1359 tipping fly ash from Chengnan power station at Wulong tip, high above Sunjiawan village and Fuxin city on 14 November 2012. As the first wagon was tilted using the loco's air pump, the fine dust initially appeared to have settled on the tip without further ado, then suddenly a dense cloud of dust eerily appeared to be rising from behind the train, and slowly continued to ascend, gradually being carried away from the city on the westerly wind. (Warwick Falconer)

Above: Beitai steelworks is around 100km south west of Shenyang, in Liaoning Province. On 10 November 2011, 1975-built SY 1077 was waiting at the No.1 Ironworks plant for molten slag to be loaded from one of the four blast furnaces there. The separate blast furnace and steel-making plants employed a fleet of 19 SYs. In 2010, around half of the fleet were still in daily use, but by early 2015 they had been usurped by diesels. (Don White)

Opposite page: The heavily polluted city of Benxi, 48km to the south east of Shenyang in Liaoning Province, is home to the Benxi Iron & Steel Company's steelworks which was originally founded in 1909. On 31 December 2004, an unidentified SY works away from between the blast furnaces with a rake of cauldron wagons. A fleet of thirty-five SYs were still required early in the new millennium for work at this plant, one of the largest steelworks in China, although diesels had already made an appearance by then. Complete dieselisation took place from January 2006, replacing the last five 'Mikados' remaining in traffic. (Don White)

One of the last remaining 762mm gauge logging lines, once widespread in North East China during the second half of the 20th century, was at Shanhetun,150km south east of Harbin in Heilongjiang Province. Tapping into the same vast forestry belt as the more well-known Weihe Forestry Railway, located 100km to the east, the Shanhetun Forestry Railway had originally been established by the Japanese, and around 420km of running lines existed at the height of production in the 1980s. The railway's main operational base was at Shanhetun, and by the 21st century the remaining line, employing a fleet of eleven C2s, followed the river valley for around 50km south east to Shahezi, where the railway split into two branch lines, each around a further 50km in length, exploiting the isolated forestry areas to the south of Weihe. On 7 March 2002, towards the end of what proved to be the railway's last logging season, *(above)* C2 No.31 arrives from the forest with a heavy train, and *(left)* timber yard pilot loco 05 is handling loaded wagons brought in overnight, the period when most of the railway's line activity would routinely take place. (All Don White)

The 762mm gauge Weihe Forestry Bureau's railway, 190km south east of Harbin in Heilongjiang Province comprised a 'main line' of just over 60km with passenger services, and additionally several branch lines solely for timber trains. On 6 January 2001, the late-running inbound 04:00 Luishan–Weihe passenger service emerges from the morning mist into a patch of weak sunlight near Zhenzhu, 6km from Weihe, with C2 No.054 heading the mixed rake comprising the system's breakdown crane and tool van, plus the passenger service coaching stock. The breakdown train had been despatched from Weihe during the previous night to deal with a derailment on the southern section.

Above: Unlike the railbus-operated passenger services, usually administered by private companies on many forestry railways in North East China, steam-hauled passenger stock was used on the Weihe Forestry Railway. On 6 January 2001, the 08:00 Weihe–Luishan service, hauled by C2 No.055, makes a spirited start away from Dongfeng station. On the northbound line, a loaded timber train is waiting to depart for Weihe. This cold, crisp, and sunny day, with a temperature of around -17C when the sun was at its zenith, was to produce an unusual procession of loaded timber trains during daylight hours, the result of a derailment during the previous day. The closure of this last steam logging railway in China at the end of the 2002–2003 season was a sad event, even documented by the Chinese media.

Opposite page: On 6 January 2001, C2 No.030 receives attention from its crew at Dongfeng station, 38km south from Weihe, whilst they wait for the arrival of the 08:00 Weihe - Luishan passenger service to clear the section.

The 762mm Huanan Coal Railway was located 70km south of Jiamusi in Heilongjiang Province. Opened in the early 1950s primarily for timber exploitation, by 1996 this had virtually ceased, but coal traffic from Hongguang colliery, 46km from Huanan, and very occasional timber, loaded at Lixin at the 36km point, ensured the railway's continuing, although precarious, survival. From an original fleet of twelve C2s, by the turn of the millennium there were seven remaining. On 30 December 2009, in the grip of an extremely severe winter, with a daytime temperature of around -30C, plus wind chill, C2 Nos.041 and 168 (not visible) struggle to make progress with a coal train across the open plain north east of Huanan, with the snow drifting across the running line, whipped up by the vicious Siberian wind. The severe conditions were expected to prevail well into 2010, and shepherds were herding their livestock from the fields towards shelter in the village of Changlonggang. After this train, the railway temporarily ceased running for several days. After leading a charmed existence for many years, the line finally succumbed to road transport in April 2011.

It was usual practice for the loco from the arriving train of empties to bank the outgoing loaded train on the steep 3km climb to the railway's summit from Lixin. On 11 November 2005, C2 No.041 is nearly over the top with a load from Hongguang. Banking loco C2 No.21043 is about to drop off and head back for the next load at the mine, as No.041 with a modest load will continue to make the sinuous descent through the forest to Tuoyaozi and on across the featureless plain to Huanan.

Left: Pyramidical waste tips loom above the traditional village of Liying in Heilongjiang Province, as Jixi Mining Administration's SY 1446 negotiates the zigzag line towards the tip and an isolated road distribution point located high above Wanjia mine and the Didao Hebei washery complex on 9 January 2010. Steam traction was last noted active on the compact Didao system in April 2011, SY 1446 being the last steam loco at Didao to work alongside the diesel newcomers, but just one year earlier it would have enjoyed the company of four further active members of its class.

Right: On 8 January 2010, SY 1544 heads away from the Xinghua mine. Steam activity on this eastern extremity of Jixi Mining Administration's Chengzihe system survived until mid-2012, finally eking out a limited existence alongside diesel traction, until completion of the electrification of the Xinghua branch. Two years earlier, a fleet of eight SYs were deployed daily about the Chengzihe system. Jixi was another of China's major coal mining centres, with collieries of varying ages and sizes dotted about, served by the mining administration's railway, on an east-west axis stretching for around 15km.

The highest daytime temperature on 3 January 2010 was -23C when Chengzihe-based SY 1058 headed a long rake of empties destined for the CNR holding sidings at Jixi Xi. Two SYs stand at the railway's main servicing and ash disposal plant at Nanchang, to the left. Discernible through the mist on the right are apartment blocks under construction, looming above the remaining rudimentary dwellings, with their fires burning. Within one year this scene would be totally transformed, the older basic housing obliterated, and the railway electrified, helping to reduce some carbon emissions in this extreme north east corner of China, 200km north of Vladivostok on the border with Russia. Limited steam operations lingered on until 2012, with just four SYs remaining active, primarily confined to working this busy section of the Chengzihe system, around the triangle of lines between Nanchang depot, Beichang washery and Dongchang mine.

Situated 60km due north of Jiamusi, 25km from the Sino-Russian border, the remarkably modern city of Hegang was another principal coal mining region in Heilongjiang Province. The extensive electrified Hegang Mining Railway system, stretching for about 25km on a north-south axis, saw nine steam-hauled passenger departures each day from the railway's central Jipei station. Even in early 2007, from a fleet of fourteen SYs, nine would see daily employment, principally on spoil trains, with one decorated and clean SY exclusively assigned to the daily passenger services. *(Above left)*: At midday on 8 January 2002 with its chime whistle echoing around the surrounding buildings, SY 0498 hurries its empty tipplers past the main shaft at Da Lu mine. *(Above right)*: Later that day viewed from atop a spoil tip at DaLu mine, the mid-afternoon sun has disappeared into the smog as the same SY returns from the spoil tipping area, heading for Nanshan Mine. *(Opposite page)*: The system's main washery was just 1km south of Jipei station, and on 5 January 2002, SYs 0683 and 0498 built Tangshan 1973 and 1972 respectively, stand alongside the facility, both with loaded spoil wagons for tipping in two separate exhausted opencast workings. Hegang's final steam duties ended in autumn 2007, replaced by diesel traction.

Shuangyashan, 50km east of Jiamusi, is a key railway hub for several deep coal mines in this extreme north east tip of Heilongjiang Province. Surrounded by small mountains bordering the Khabarovsk and Primorsky Krai states of Russia, the city's name, bestowed in 1384 during the Ming Dynasty, translates as the 'twin ducks mountains', named after two peaks, north east of the city. The city became part of the Japanese puppet state of Manchukuo upon invasion by the Japanese in 1931, but during the 2nd World War the Soviet Army, aided by the Chinese communists, defeated the Japanese occupiers, and Heilongjiang became the first province under communist control. Rich in coal and other minerals, the population of the town expanded considerably after the exploitation of extensive coal mining from the late 1950s, much of its coal output supplying the vast Anshan Steelworks. The winters are long and bitterly cold, averaging between -30C and -15C in January. Many of the Shuangyashan Coal Railway's fleet of fifteen former CNR QJs and ten SYs were worked intensively right up until dieselisation of the entire system on 26 March 2002. The QJs were used on passenger and freight diagrams, with the SYs usually employed on shorter trip workings, shunting, and on a solitary branch-line passenger service at Dianchang. Passenger services from Shuangyashan Zhongxin station on the Fushan line, and along the longer Shuangxing line, comprised up to eleven coaches, deplorably grimy outside and filthy internally, with leisurely single journey times of around 1½ and 2 hours duration respectively. The exchange yard is adjacent to the city's CNR station, and alongside this yard was the steam loco running depot, complete with a wall for 'blowing down', where a lethal skating rink for the unwary would almost instantaneously be topped up with ice from departing locos during the depths of winter. A steeply graded line, seeing only freight traffic and light loco movements, ran south from the CNR exchange yard to Zhongxin station. The system at the turn of the century served around ten major coal mines, the city's power station, and a modern power plant at Bafengchang (aka Dianchang). The railway bore a remarkable resemblance to a remote outpost of the state railway, particularly with its frequent, lengthy, and well patronised QJ-hauled passenger trains. Loaded coal trains, sometimes double-headed and/or banked, and passenger services, were as a rule worked tender-first into Shuangyashan.

Left: On 30 December 2000, alongside the single platform of Zhongxin station, Tangshan works 1972-built SY 0597 draws away, having deposited a single gondola wagon requiring works attention, before returning to the city's power station to collect a complete rake of empties.

Left: Leaving a curved exhaust trail in its wake, Shuangyashan's 1985-built QJ 6917 lifts a long rake of gondola wagons, some sheeted, out of the CNR exchange yard during the mid-morning of 2 January 2001. The unusually clear sunlight in the -40C temperature perfectly illuminated only the chosen location for capturing this awe-inspiring departure.

Right: On 2 January 2001, Tangshan 1973-built SY 0632 brings two loaded wagons up into Shuangyashan yard from the steelworks branch line on the south west fringe of the city. An elderly gent cautiously picks his way along the icy track, descending past basic dwellings and local shops, whose days are numbered like the 'Mikado'. This area was subsequently transformed with new high-rise apartments, replacing the uniform basic housing, and a dual-carriageway road now crosses the railway by means of an overbridge, where the rear wagon is located.

Above: On the morning of 1 January 2001, in a temperature of around -40C, Datong works 1982-built QJ 3593 receives attention from the crew at Shuangyashan's servicing point. As the loco takes on water, the hapless shed labourers break up the ice quickly forming around the servicing pits.

Left: A labourer battles against the harsh conditions on the morning of 1 January 2001, removing ash from within and around the disposal pit, before it rapidly transforms into an immovable frozen lump. Soon after its workshop visit, and smelling of freshly applied paint, Shuangyashan's 1985-built QJ 7020 sets back into the depot servicing area. Unusually facing north, it would soon be turned to face in the same direction as all of the other fleet members, and it would most probably have been the last loco on the system to receive a heavy overhaul.

Viewed across the rooftops of some basic residential dwellings on Shuangyashan's southern outskirts, the sun gradually dips into the smog on 31 December 2000, as 1984-built QJ 6805 heads the 14:40 Shuangyashan–Dongbaowei passenger service away from the city, the last outbound passenger diagram on this branch before withdrawal of its passenger services entirely.

On 3 January 2002, 1983-built QJ 3598 passes through Qixing mine, heading the 12:30 Shuangyashan - Shuangxing passenger service comprising eleven coaches and totalling 550 tonnes gross. The balanced return working from wind-swept Shuangxing would steam into Shuangyashan Zhongxin at 18:18, but only for another three months, after which diesel traction would take over.

The large opencast mine at Jalainur (aka Zhalainuoer), affectionately named 'the big pit', would have been high on the wish list for any steam enthusiast's first visit to China from around the late 1990s, certainly before news of another large opencast operation at Sandaoling became known in railway circles. The Jalainur Mining Railway, in Inner Mongolia, was 29km south east of the Sino-Russian border town of Manzhouli. It was one of the greatest steam spectacles in the world at the time, perhaps second only to the much loved and visited JiTong provincial railway, with its fleet of around 100 QJs. However, the breath-taking spectacle of so many SY 'Mikados' at Jalainur making zigzag ascents and descents with their trains in and around the massive opencast pit was a sight unequalled anywhere else in the world, and no single photo can do it justice, nor to the thrill anyone would have experienced on a visit there. Jalainur's railway layout evolved over time, both within the opencast and around the washery, especially in the immediate Dongfanghong washery area, where the interchange sidings had been raised, resulting in a tough climb for locos from the complex with a dead load, sometimes requiring banking, double-heading, or splitting of the train. The entire layout at Jalainur was virtually unrecognisable in 2009 in comparison with a decade earlier. But even during the final months of steam operations there, it was still possible to see up to eighteen SYs working in the 'big pit' at any one time. Additionally, the Mining Railway was also responsible for the rail traffic supporting several deep mines, a power station, and a washery, as well as providing two separate workers' 'paddy' trains around the system, each comprising a single coach. The railway had a well-equipped workshop where all but the heaviest of repairs could be undertaken on its fleet of around fifty SY locos. Even in 2006, up to thirty SYs would be active at any one time around the system. The first diesel locos began to arrive at Jalainur in February 2009, and were immediately put to work on trains serving the deep mines, in what proved to be the final year for regular steam operations, when the railway in the opencast pit was replaced by dumper trucks, and the track quickly removed.

Right: A remarkable coming-together of three SYs at Jalainur opencast coal mine on 9 March 2009, when the three locos, all moving, came into line with each other momentarily as they made their way along various levels of the mine's crater. The juxtaposition was not pre-arranged, and the photographer remarks that he watched spellbound with fingers crossed for several minutes as the possibility of a three-way line-up began to emerge. (Nick Pigott)

A scene on 9 January 2009, from the eastern rim looking into the 'big pit' – two unidentified SYs are moving from the pit's maintenance area, 'Station 510 ' to different work faces, both with a fixed rake of six tippler wagons ready for loading. A single passenger coach from the 'paddy' train was held there between services. This was the local servicing point, which obviated the need for locos with their fixed wagon rakes to make the time consuming and zig-zagging journey out of the opencast pit for their daily running maintenance, coaling and watering. (Don White)

Dongfanghong washery at Jalainur on 7 January 2009, during its last year of steam working, with the regular loco used on the washery duties, smoke deflector-fitted SY 1416 hard at work in a -30C temperature. (Don White)

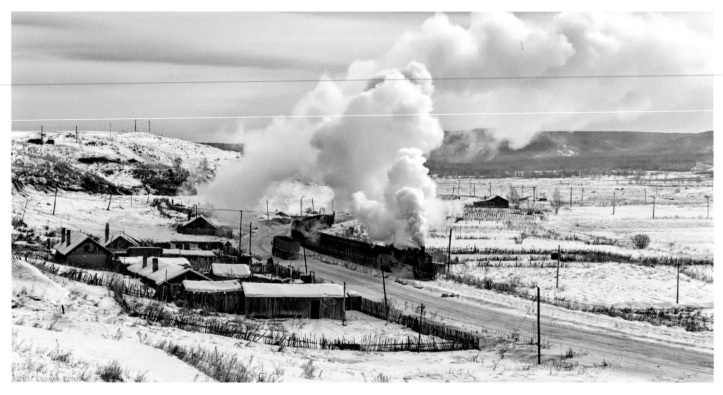

On 21 February 2017, Tangshan works 1983-built SY 1225 was hard at work on the branch between Wujiu and No.3 mine, one of four connected to this isolated system. The Wujiu Mining Railway, centrally located in Inner Mongolia, 1,300km directly north east of Beijing and 680km from Harbin, is a typical and quite unremarkable rural colliery railway system in a remote setting, with basic uniform housing and smallholdings characteristically hugging its running lines, which were in recent years worked by a solitary SY from a fleet of three. So many systems akin to this sole survivor were once widespread in China, many ignored by visiting enthusiasts in the past, some not even documented at all, especially when more rewarding concentrations of steam activity could be enjoyed elsewhere in the limited time available to most visitors. It is therefore quite fitting that such an understated steam-worked operation should survive for so long into the 21st century, receiving celebrity status purely by virtue of its survival. With the grip of the coronavirus pandemic restricting world travel from early 2020, and with additional travel restrictions imposed within China itself, steam operations at this extreme outpost, already infiltrated by a solitary DF4 diesel by 2016, came to an unrecorded end around September 2021. When the fires are finally thrown out of the handful of surviving JS 'Mikados' working on Sandaoling's Nanzhan to Erzhan deep mines' branch line, that really will be the end of industrial steam in China, but it is quite remarkable and fitting that a few of the last survivors there would originally have seen service on main line metals in Gansu Province, when first delivered to CNR from the Datong works in the late 1980s. (Darryl Bond)